SALON SAMPLER©

FROM THE SALON PUNK

Alan Forrest Smith

"THE SALON IS CHANGING ... PHONE HAS NEVER STOPPED ... JUST INSANE"

Well, what can I say!!

We had a salon, a team, a business – Or so we thought!!

We were taking on average £2-3000 a week, it covered the bills... just! We spent A LOT of nights worrying about how we were going to pay the staff if there was money in the bank to pay the product company.... We didn't take a wage, we didn't have any spare cash, we thought we were doing everything like we should but we were still not seeing any increase.... until we called Alan.

We spent many more nights wondering whether we should take the risk, it was a lot of money that we certainly didn't have.

We made the jump... and it was honestly THE BEST THING WE HAVE EVER DONE!!!!

Alan ripped our business apart and showed us it in a completely different light....

In 4 weeks he has refocused our attention on stabilizing and building a BUSINESS.

He has almost DOUBLED our turnover in 4 weeks....... at the quietest time of the year!!

He has opened our eyes to everything about our business and what we were doing and has flipped it on its head!!

It's INTENSE, ITS HARD WORK AND ITS EXTREME!! But we are ABSOLUTELY LOVING IT!! The results are UNREAL....

We are 4 weeks in.....we can't for the results after 12.

Alan is fantastic, he is supportive, encouraging and he knows what he's talking about! He is ALWAYS at the end of the phone, he keeps us focused and he gets results...... it 's just simply amazing!

I can't wait to write about our journey after the next 4 weeks!

WE CANT THANK YOU ENOUGH.......SIMPLY AMAZING!!!!!

Rich and Steph, Sage Hair Wickham

I can hardly believe THE CHANGE in not only my business but in ME.

Alan's strategies and advice with guidance took my business to a 53.4% rise in one month, 116% rise in one year. It would have been more but I had to make HUGE decisions along the way to create the hairdressing salon of my dreams which meant having the confidence to make changes and get the people out who I knew deep down were not right for me and my business in the long term.

I don't know how long it would have taken me to make these changes without Alan's support. 'GO FOR IT. (if ever)

With Alan's support, I made the changes and STILL made the 116% growth.

I have taken what Alan has taught me with my own skills and knowledge and have not only taken my business to near full capacity but he have given me a better understanding of business and I am just about to launch 2 big projects out with the salon.

I now have the confidence and knowledge to push my career forward and create the work life I want… He has GENIUS IDEAS that were so inspiring I didn't take much time to get excited and start putting them into action.

Caroline Sanderson, Ego Hair Inverness, Scotland

"Two Salons DOUBLED new clients" – Simon, ZigZag Salon Group

They say there's no school like the old skool and Alan is definitely the headmaster of the hairdressing industry and since working with Alan even though we were a little shocked at what he was asking us to do however we implement what he asked and are now starting to see results and can see the light at the end of the tunnel with two of our salons doubling their new clients to 17%."

Simon Hayter, CEO ZigZag Hairdressing Group

Honestly, Alan has helped us focus and given us belief.

Don't get me wrong, it's been really hard but rewarding work !! Alan has been there constantly in the background cajoling, demanding, driving and giving us ideas and has been on hand 24hrs a day!

He is true to his word. Honest as hell and a great guy that wants you to succeed at all times.

I think any business will benefit from working with Alan.

Izaak Brading & James Langley

Mod Salons, Leeds

"INSPIRATIONAL"

"Alan is an inspirational leader."

Not a leader who seeks power or glory, but a true leader who is uplifted by the achievements of others; those he has lifted from failure, or frustration, or those trapped in the treacle of life.

He is business clever. Not many can visualise a dud business in three dimensions, turning the company in his mind, penetrating to the bowels, foreseeing the traps, and laying an imaginative path towards its success.

This is not something that can be taught at university; it is inbuilt into the DNA of a privileged few. And if they also have that rare gift… the ability to teach with clarity and humour…then what you have is Alan Forrest Smith. It has been a privilege to know and work with Alan.

David Nore, Australia

CONTENTS

SALON SAMPLER - THE BREAKTHROUGH PROGRAM THAT EVERY SALON SHOULD BE DOING

Do this and you will be light years ahead of all of your competition.

Dear Salon Owner

This is Alan The Salon Punk here.

I get asked this a lot.

'Alan if you had to do just one thing to pack out any salon what would it be?'

Interesting question in a time where I meet salon owners that want more and more of new things that work when in actual fact is it possible to do just one thing so brilliantly well – it is all you need?

I know the answer because the answer is the single most effective column building strategy I have used myself for well over 17-years to take my own salons to Number one. To pack out all of my stylists and keep them packed from week-to-week for years!

Here is that one brilliant strategy that I would still make a priority to use today and I promise you if you do it properly, if you listen closely and **IF** you stick to the simple punk rules I put down for you, there is a huge chance it could transform your salon very quickly or even faster!

I will go a step further and say this… This program will very easily increase your salon client list and columns by 25% in a single week if you stick to the simple rules.

Let me share this, SALON SAMPLER breakthrough column building program comes with two initial thoughts.

The first being that this can very easily transform your client list faster than you will ever believe. Everyone will tell you not to do this this. That is the best reason you should be doing it … you'll be and will be the one and only taking a measured risk like this.

The second thought is this and comes with a warning: If you fail to understand everything I am about to share with you it might and it could end in disaster. Stick to what I tell you, ignore those that advise otherwise, this is tested and works!

And don't shake with fear just yet because there is even better news and it is this. You don't have hundreds of new things to learn. This isn't about a new computer program or any other technical marketing tool that you need to be a scientist to understand. It isn't about an overweight corporate expert in an aging grey suit, shirt and tie trying to train hairdressers about something he really can never understand or a new five-minute expert (guru) with a half decent idea they copied from a book they read just before bed time.

What you are about to discover is the answer to this question I was asked at the start …

'Alan if you had to do just one thing to pack out any salon what would it be?'

SALON SAMPLER – **IS** That Program

The first thing I want to advise you to do is read everything about SALON SAMPLER twice. Once you have read this book I want to ask you to read it again. Why? So, you get it.

As a hairdresser, myself the last thing I was interested in was numbers or business strategy. But I was interested in getting more. The problem is we really need to know the numbers if we want more. So, I have kept the numbers side as light as I can for you and of course for me. (the truth is numbers bore me to death until I see my bank statement then I get interested)

There are rules for SALON SAMPLER. You need to stick to the rules. The rules are there to protect and build your client list. If you have more clients you have more cash in your bank account. If you have more cash in your bank you are a happier salon owner that for sure. The rules are also part of a tested program. I have tested SALON SAMPLER in my own salons and in many salons since.

SALON SAMPLER is in three main parts.

- The understanding (getting your head around that you are not doing services for FREE)
- The consultation (critical part that turns all samples into cash for your salon)
- The process (what and how to do what you need to do)

Within each section there are smaller sections you should take notice of also. The smaller parts are all designed to support the bigger part or the bigger idea. DON'T panic everything is a piece of cake. Doing it is the tough bit!

But again, let's not confuse this too much. This is all about one big idea – SALON SAMPLER - that could change your salon and your columns forever. By the way I ran this every week from the early days of opening my salons until I sold them in 2003 (17-years). Why? Because the impact is so dramatic at every level, it's fast, it is super-effective and it works.

And a short story.

Helen was a bitch. In the salon, she created trouble for me at every level. She was the one that would sit with her face in a newspaper or magazine at the desk. She was the one that the young staff looked up to. She was the one that resisted every single thing I would ask my team to do. And when I was not around she was the one that would tell everyone that everything I was doing in my salon was a waste of time.

When I began to do samples she actually got my team together when I wasn't in the salon and told all of them they should not be doing anything for free. She even went a step further and asked everyone to walk out of the salon if we were asked to do it. I was eventually told about this little rebellion and managed to squash it. The reality was she was lazy, wanted to start late, have long lunches and leave early with her boyfriend. She also had seen my sampling tests in the salon and saw the volume of new clients coming into the salon using it. The last thing she wanted was more clients and to be busier. My staff loved doing it and I finally fired her after all she was actually actively trying to destroy my salon.

What a huge variety of reasons you will have certain staff that will resist your efforts. Some very publicly and some very sneakily away from your face.

Stick to this – it works. And if you have to and can – fire the trouble makers, they do not deserve your commitment, love and hard efforts in your business.

So please, please, please do not miss out anything and for god's sake stop listening to opinions from those that haven't got a clue.

OK? Let's do this.

There's No Such Thing As Free Hairdressing.

In 1991, I had moved into my second and new salon. My first salon was just 250 sq. ft. It was pretty small. My 2nd salon was a huge 2000 sq. ft. And frankly, I nearly blew it in the very early days.

I had 6 stylists and 2 juniors but really we just didn't have the clients coming through despite being on a pretty busy street and next to a 4 car park and the biggest super market in the town. It just wasn't happening.

This meant that I was paying staff with money I wasn't taking to stand around to do nothing. They did stand around doing nothing, drunk tea and coffee at my expense, read newspapers at the desk as well as eat endlessly, talk, gossip moan until they got bored and then left for another salon or I had to let them go. Looking back, I don't blame them.

Then one day something happened at home that inspired me and made me think about the effect this thing could have in my salon: I received some small butter samples through my letter box. I actually grew up on very salty butter in Scotland but in England from the age of seven we never really had butter. As an adult, I'd never really bought butter at all. It was always given a bad press due to being just too hard on the heart and cholesterol. I was always a margarine man and nothing would change that. I can be a little fixated on things like that. I am the type of guy that is very loyal and rarely breaks that disloyalty when I am happy with a service. Get me in, look after me and I am the perfect customer for life (upset me though and you'll never see me again).

Anyway, the butter samples came again and again-more butter samples with slightly different offers and wrappings. Still the same brand of butter all the same. I am also very by nature very curious so one day rather than just throw them in the rubbish with all the other flyers and sales letter that came through the door I decided to try the butter on my toast rather than the margarine. I did and I absolutely loved the butter. The next time we went shopping was the first time we bought the big tub of the same brand of free sample butter I'd been getting through the post (LUR-PAK). Obviously, we paid and to this day I still use the same brand of butter.

The butter company had stolen me as a long-term paying customer from the margarine company and I would now buy their butter (as I still do today).

This was because of a **SAMPLE** (not free) that obviously cost the company money to to send to me and probably millions of others.

This small sample got me thinking about how I could offer samples into my salons. If I had bought butter and been persuaded to change my brand on the basis of a tiny free sample could I do the same thing in my salons? Not send butter but send out salon samples.

The fact is LURPAK butter didn't give me anything for free. They gave me a sample. That sample will have cost them cash to mail out to me. I eventually used that sample and then went to the supermarket to buy their butter. That was in 1989 and I am still using that butter today. The sample was free but imagine how much I have spent with the butter company since 1989? They had taken me from my margarine company and I am today a loyal paying customer. It wasn't free … it was a sample to get me to buy from them.

Could I get other salon's loyal clients to come into my salon using a SAMPLE? So, all the way back to 1990 I decided to create a free sample cut and finish service in my samples.

In those days, I didn't over think it. It was simply FREE Hairdressing. The client stayed or went, but it felt good doing loads of samples because the salon looked packed. Until that is...

... One day in the salon there was a local vagrant having his haircut. The smell was insane and at the time I really just didn't want him in the salon. His hair was also packed with lice. This wasn't uncommon with FREE. Another time we had a group of Irish travelers in the salon (Note: I love the Irish). Not only did all 15 of them get their haircut FREE they did their best to empty my shelves without paying on the way out.

My own thoughtless version of FREE haircutting was a expensive mess. My staff and me would simply give away haircuts for all that took the flyer out of our hands and we serviced them on myself on the basis that the client would like us and come back again. They didn't.

In some but in very few cases it worked well. When it worked well it was almost by accident. Most of the time doing FREE and simply hoping client's return is a huge mistake as I found out.

I discovered ...

- There had to be a really strong plan to sampling

- There had to be a really good reason to give out any kind of sample
- There had to be a really good goal behind doing sampling
- It had to be tracked, measured and calculated properly
- Every free service had to sell something like colour, restyle or hair product

Free samples had to be very carefully thought out from start to finish or they could destroy my salon.

And let me emphasise this again … MOST STAFF HATED doing anything FREE. They would tell me they were artists not salesmen and just didn't want to do it. They just never understood the bigger picture. They never understood because I never explained it to them. They didn't get it and frankly I don't think I did at the time, it just felt like a decent idea.

So, my new sampling adventure had to be fixed or dropped otherwise not only was it all for nothing but it could potentially destroy my salon business very fast (I once had a Saturday in my salon with around ten FREE haircuts. Because of them we turned away paying clients – dangerous!).

Eventually, after giving away literally dozens and maybe hundreds of haircuts I realised we were not getting many any clients back into the salon. The staff couldn't care less because they were still getting paid their wages and I was freaking out seeing a lot of haircuts for free with no money coming into the drawer. (you know that moment where you pay everyone – only just – on a Saturday and you have nothing to pay yourself!)

FREE haircuts were almost a huge disaster for my salons.

The reason I want to really emphasis this is that you might already be doing some kind of free sample program. You might also be getting advice to avoid this strategy by someone. Yet it can be amazing as long as it carefully controlled otherwise it could destroy your business.

FREE is not the same as discounting. I want you to know long term discounting your salon will destroy your business. It creates a mindset in your clients or potential new clients that you are cheap, they will always get their hair lower if they hold on for a discount and that frankly can look a little desperate. SALON SAMPLER program isn't about discounting but there is no comparison to sampling and discounting.

So here are the critical things I discovered during my own sampling period that you need to take notice of.

Once you know these things, the SALON SAMPLER program will show you how to create a SALON SAMPLER (Free Hairdressing) program that will build your salon like never before. If you use SALON SAMPLER as the only tool to build your salon business, when done right it will perform like nothing else in your salon ever. And I should know because I've done it in my own salons for almost 17-years and many other salons I have worked with since then. IT WORKS!

Next, here are my TEN COMMANDMENTS of SALON SAMPLER PROGRAM. Break them at your own risk!

Print them out and stick them on your office wall.

The 10 Commandments of SALON SAMPLER

1. SALON SAMPLER is a sample program NOT a FREE program – There is a huge difference
2. You must never say out loud SALON SAMPLER this a free program
3. You must adhere to the SALON SAMLER rules at all time
4. You must never do SALON SAMPLER as a random act of desperation
5. You must plan SALON SAMPLER and stick to the plan
6. You must practice SALON SAMPLER before you start it
7. You must never allow anyone untrained to use SALON SAMPLER

8. You must track and measure the results from every SALON SAMPLER campaign
9. You must stop any stylist that uses SALON SAMPLER that fails to get results – they are missing something – it isn't the program
10. You must not take the name of SALON SAMPLER in vain – I know what works so just do it.

THE UNDERSTANDING: Understand the proven reasons before starting your SALON SAMPLER

You have to have a good reason for doing SALON SAMPLER. Saying I want 'Katie' busy isn't a good enough reason. She could be busy all day doing nothing in particular with sampling.

It is important when you do any sampling that you have a longer term or bigger goal for your salon.

When I began my own sampling program I finally realised I had to and then did work out the numbers. The numbers that each stylist had to deliver each day. I knew this because I also knew how much they had to deliver into the salon annually through their column. Once I knew the annual number I divided that number by 48 weeks. I then had a weekly number I could then again divide by 5 working days and that gave me a number that each stylist had to generate daily. To make this easier again I always gave my staff a number for AM. And PM. Or in other words a number they had to generate in the morning and then in the afternoon. This kept the understanding of numbers as simple as possible for staff and myself.

If you tell your staff you want them to take £68,452 per year (a year's takings I n the stylist column) they will just freak out. If you tell them you want £142.60 in the morning and then the afternoon, it sounds easy and do-able. The daily numbers is the annual number divided by 48 weeks.

SALON SAMPLER NUMBERS: TWO NEW CLIENTS DAILY

I cannot say this enough – it is critical you know your numbers. I remember taking businesses courses many years ago. During this course, someone would start talking numbers. My first reaction when anyone talks about numbers is to daydream or literally fall asleep. My mind cannot get into them. They would be helping me create a salon that would be successful by knowing my numbers. I would have even paid for that yet while the speaker was talking numbers I was dreaming about saving the universe. Numbers used to be a huge turn off now your salon numbers – and if you are turned off by numbers like I am it doesn't matter – you must find these out for successful sampling program.

Let's create an example to make this really simple.

All the numbers are just examples. Your salon might be lower or much higher.

Your salon takings are currently at £100,000 per annum.

You would like your salon takings to get to £150,000 per annum.

See how this is very doable with Salon Sampler.

Let's say your average bill per client is £75.

Now divide the (extra) £50,000 that you want by your average bill of £75.

This means to hit your goal you need 666 new clients per year into your salon. Sounds a lot right but it isn't – watch this.

666 (clients) divided by 48-weeks (working salon weeks) is 14 new clients per week.

14 divided by 6 (days) is just over 2 clients.

In other words, here is what you need to do to hit your goal of £50,000

Just TWO NEW clients each day both spending on average £75.

But Alan aren't we doing these clients for FREE or giving them a sample?

NO

NO

NO

No, you are forgetting the first commandment of Salon Sampler – there is no such thing as free – this is a sample. Once they get a sample and love it they come back for more.

Now here's the really cool thing.

You see the number above of 666 clients per year?

That isn't quite true. I lied, kind of.

The reason is this.

The number 666 are clients that become regular clients.

Let's say as an average they visit and pay four visits into your salon per year (average is actually around five visits). This now means the number 666 are visits the real number of clients is just 167 new clients needed annually to increase your salon turnover by £50,000.

In other words, the number 666 is divided by four.

Now we also know the average client make five visits a year. I said four because the first visit they come for they don't pay – this is their sample.

See how easy it is once you know the numbers? There is more to come later in this little book of course, but because I already told you, unless salon sampler is part of a system, it can destroy your salon.

So, although knowing your numbers is good at this stage it still isn't good enough. For now, you need to do this.

Write down the following

What is the new salon turnover you would like to hit?

What is your salon average bill?

Number of clients you need per annum?

How many clients daily?

How many clients in the morning?

How many clients in the afternoon?

PART 1. FREE is not free when it's a SALON SAMPLE

I go to Yoga and use a class close to where I live. So, close in fact it's around 5-minute walk. I've gone there with my wife for a while now.

Recently a new Yoga place opened in the next town. I'd seen it but had been there. It's been open for a few months.

Recently we walked past and noticed they had a free trial class advertised in the window (sample). We went in and signed up for the trial despite feeling a bit bad because of our loyalty to the other teachers at the other classes we go to.

I wasn't sure about going because I have been to a ton of Yoga classes in many places all over the world and after many years now realise the class being called a yoga class doesn't mean the teacher will be any good. So, when I find a class I enjoy I rarely change my loyalty.

Anyway, this time I did, we did change our loyalty. We went on the sample yoga class, loved the sample and have been going to these classes since (over a year as I write). Our previous local yoga class have now lost customers (and the revenue from me and my wife) and this new place has won a loyal and new customer from an initial sample.

How?

The class we used go to is just a white multi-purpose room above a gym. There are no curtains. It can be cold in winter and doesn't really heat up. There is no real 'yogi' atmosphere but the classes are good (once you warm up) and the teachers are mostly really great. But it's just a yoga class in a room – that's it!

When we went to the new yoga classes there were more than a few things in place that made us stay and won us as new customers from the sample.

- The room décor and atmosphere was done wonderfully.
- The lightening system was amazing.
- The teachers are excellent and clearly well trained.
- The staff were really very smiley and well trained.

- The receptionist was great.
- They have a small food and drink part.
- They had an amazing waiting area.
- The changing rooms are clean.
- They offer showers.
- It was very hot (hot yoga).

But most of all for me the whole thing feels more like a 'yogi' experience rather than a yoga class in a room that is used for many other things.

The class itself was packed to the hilt and is always packed every time we go.

We have now spent a lot of money with them every week and every month.

The classes are higher priced than where we usually go (£3 at our old class and £12 at the new class).

They email us and I love reading their emails.

They text us to send offers or class reminders.

They have a booking App that is as simple as a single click.

It's all very slick.

It's all very cool.

In other words, …

They blew us away on THE FREE VISIT and have been blowing us away since. The perfect SAMPLE! (IMPORTANT: Once you set up for an amazing service it is essential you don't let that service slip. It will now and then of course but push to keep it high)

FREE is NOT free and in salon sampler we are not allowed to use the word free. The first visit was free but now we spend £12 per class twice a week. That is £2,400 per year they didn't have before they gave us the samples. If they do that with fifty people that is £60,000 from sampling alone. Imagine that in your salon?

The yoga class gave us a sample and we loved what we got once we used the sample despite the future price being higher than what we already pay elsewhere.

And remember – price is rarely an issue to a happy customer.

I recently got a free pen in the mail. I have done a lot of mailing and sending letters over the years in my own businesses. It isn't cheap. Can you imagine sending 25,000 letters that include a pen in the envelope? I would guess maybe £70,000 costs just to send a mail and letter like this. Anyway, the pen arrived in a nice high-end envelope. It had a first class postage. It came with a long letter about how great their pens are (I didn't read it). I took the pen and threw away the long letter.

The pen is very good, looks great in silver with gold finish. It is quite thick unlike a cheap pen and writes very nicely. That was around two years ago. They are probably expecting me to buy more.

The reality is this.

They wasted their money because they didn't have a system in place before or after they sent me the sample. I have no idea now who the pen came from or where to buy another. Here's the crazy thing, if I knew where it had come from I would have bought more.

Someone in their office decided to do FREE sample rather than real sampling and that free will kill their business.

See the difference between the Yoga Company and the Pen Company?

SAMPLE: The Yoga Company gave a SAMPLE… I bought more. They keep in touch weekly and let me know how to buy my next classes.

FREE: The Pen company gave away FREE… I didn't buy anything. They never once got in touch with me after they sent the pen.

In my salons, I eventually had a very strict sampling policy. It had to be because so much can go wrong when doing free samples (like Saturday being packed with free haircuts). Don't worry, next I will show you how to do SAMPLING at it's very best.

So ask yourself this question.

Why do you want to do a salon sampler program? You must know the reason.

Do you know your numbers? If you don't know them – you are screwed!

Do you know what the outcome is going to be? When designed well the program will give you a predictable outcome.

How will doing a sample program affect your salon? It will affect your whole salon not just the stylist doing it so think through the effect of the program.

How will it affect your turnover? For good or bad?

How will doing salon sampler affect your team? They will react in ways you don't expect.

What is the outcome you want? Do you know? If not stop right now.

An example or two of Salon Sampler in action.

Example: I had a new stylist start in my salon. She arrived with all the usual promises of clients but of course brought just one or two.

I decided to put her on a SALON SAMPLER program.

Now, before I go into what I did I made sure the stylist knew exactly what the purpose of sampling is. I will warn you – if you don't explain this to them fully they will just do free hairdressing rather than a sampling program.

You should know I meet a lot of salon owners that are slightly fearful of their staff so they step around on tiptoes rather than tell the staff to their faces.

To create a successful business, you have to be firm, resolute and make sure they understand exactly what you are doing with the sampler program.

Here's' how.

Explain the program in detail to them.

Tell them the benefits for them personally.

Ask them to repeat it back.

Get them to write out the program in their words and ask them to sign it as an agreement.

1. The first thing I wanted it to do was cover her wages and my costs.

2. The second thing was I worked out how many salon samplers I wanted her to do each week and tell her my expectations.
3. The third thing was to measure any upsells coming into the salon from the sampler.
4. The fourth thing was to check the consultation was being done properly (all samples were expected to upsell, advice and consult fully.
5. And finally, I made sure that not single sampler client left the salon without – SPENDING some money (this isn't hard sell its advising properly).

So, I sat her down and started the explanation. I explained to her like this.

"I am going to start you on a SAMPLING program. This means you are offering a sample of your brilliant work but I need you to remember that this isn't about giving away a free haircut this is about winning over a client. This means if you book her in for a free haircut you need to blow her away. The only way you will blow her away is by doing something that she isn't getting at her current salon. This means you should focus on change and advising her with restyling, colour and home haircare. Show her your skills but show her you care about how she looks and feels from start to finish.

This means for you if you do this right you will increase your column very very quickly. After 8-12 weeks you will be a lot busier and this also means you will be getting paid more money. The more clients you do the more I can pay you.

I also expect the client to spend some money after her sample. Either for color, other services, hair care. I want to see some sale from the sample client. Does this make sense?

Now I am paying you £300 per week. I need you to take at least £500 per week right away. Once you hit £500 this covers employing you. To start hitting commissions we need to get your salon takings to at least £900. After this I can start to pay you more and give you more of what you need in from your work here.

Now from every sample you do I need to see…

Restyling, colour sales, haircare sales and rebooking. And of course, we will measure all of the referrals you do with every sample client.

Now I want you to do this for me. Explain to me what you will be doing and I also need you to write out what you are going to do and how you are going to do this?"

Sounds easy I know but actually it is easier for you if you remain firm and stick to the plan (detailed later).

I spoke to a salon owner that was terrified if telling his staff to do this. He told me staff just don't want to do anything he tells them anyway. If you feel like this don't worry it is common. If staff are a problem you need to know how to replace them and then hire staff that are willing to work in your system. Staff of course are a whole other story. As a salon owner you must remain in control of your business. Once your staff control everything you are in trouble but this can be fixed with a new strategy.

So back to the stylist: After she agreed she was allocated a fixed amount of sampling vouchers/flyers daily. We started her on just 10. This meant she was personally responsible for handing out ten samples each day. At the end of the day the samples were counted. If she had eight left clearly, she wasn't doing it. If she had zero she had done an amazing job. If she had ten remaining … we had a major problem.

All the samples were done using paper NOT digital. The response rate climbs using paper. It gets forgotten using digital.

From the 10 samples, I would expect 3 to come into my salon. And you should expect the same. I have seen them as high as 6 from 10 but never 10-10. Be realistic some people will never be persuaded even with a free option.

Now the key to this is of course the consultation.

SALON SAMPLER: The Consultation

Now like all things there is a key to SALON SAMPLER and that key is good training and of course a good personality with the new team member you choose. If you employ someone with a face like a smacked backside they will always have a face like a smacked backside. This is where you must refine your interview process and choose the right staff.

But the key beyond this is a strong, well trained and powerful consultation. If they simply hand out samples and do not take time to deliver a strong consultation the sample WILL FAIL.

Let's take one step back a little here.

How does your client think and feels about coming to a new salon?

Let's assume this is a woman. She has been using another hairdresser for over 15-years. She was handed a

SAMPLE on the street, she is nervous to the point of freaking out over coming into a new salon. Her old salon is familiar even the owners dog that walks around knows her. Your salon isn't familiar; she knows nothing apart from what she read in your salon sampler flyer.

This is what her mind goes through.

Based on your flyer and her online research through Facebook, Instagram, your website and reviews online she has made a choice to call you. Seconds before the call she is nervous.

Based on how you react on that telephone or email reply she makes another decision. That is are you going to be any good or do you sound like just any other salon.

The day she comes to your salon she will be nervous. She is nervous when she sees your salon and will have a butterfly in her belly that's for sure. On approaching your salon, she is almost terrified of opening the salon front door but when she enters remember she has never been before so is a little unsure what to do and who to speak to. How you all react at this point will give her enough information to decide are you any good or not and will she stay or even come back.

As she sits and waits although she pretends to read she is watching everything, looking at everything and making judgments on your staff, your skills, your services and your salon. She is watching the way you handle hair and treat clients because she knows she is next.

She is still very nervous. If her hair isn't right it could take months to grow out. Finally, someone comes to move her from the reception into the salon. She does feel slightly intimidated and uneasy. If the staff don't make her feel at ease again she will judge your salon and maybe never return. It isn't uncommon for sample clients to be treated as 2nd class by staff so be careful they know that although she is a salon sampler she is also VIP.

The stylist can react in two ways to their new client.

One: simply get her hair washed and processed and then speak to her from behind the chair.

Two: Introduce himself properly, sit with the client, treat her like a human being, a friend and a highly valued sampler client that they will bend over backwards to get an incredible result for her.

Either way the client will still feel nervous, will talk relatively quiet and is still a little unsure of what to say or do.

Don't forget her previous stylist has done her hair for over 10-years. It has taken a lot for her to come to you. She has come so far based on your SALON SAMPLER

PROGRAM, her telephone call into your salon and now how the team treats her whilst in your salon. Are you starting to see how critical it is for you to train your team properly in salon welcoming and consulting?

So here are what you must do to make sure the consultation is an all-powerful tool within your salon and remember – your staff most of the time WILL NOT want to do this so you must manage, coach and guide your team at all times. When I say all times, I mean every day you should or your manager should keep on top of this.

So, check this always …

Make sure they know the new clients name in advance from the appointment book.

Introduce themselves (stylists) to the new client

Put the client at ease

Use light welcoming conversation to start with

Reassure the client about the salon and skills

Ask the client what problems they might have with their hair?

Ask the client the last time they changed their hair?

Ask the client what the worst thing could be from today?

Ask the client if they can handle their hair at home themselves?

Ask the client if they want a total make-over?

Ask the client how much time they spend daily on their hair?

Ask the client to show you how they dry their hair at home?

Ask the client if they have a favorite famous hairstyle they'd love?

Ask the client to show you the last hairstyle they'd ever want?

Ask the client what they definitely do not want today?

Ask what products they use at home?

Ask what tools they have at home?

And ask all the relevant questions needed.

Before doing anything, the stylist should then say to the client something like…

"I have listened to everything we have spoken about and here is what I suggest" … the stylist then offers a suggestion for the sampler client's hair.

Now the client has booked in for a haircut only so this is your team's opportunity to upsell service (if they need it – no if they don't). Most hairdressers would agree hair needs a little more but rarely will they suggest it unless the client asks. It is critical that the stylist makes the suggestion.

Once the stylist has listened as part of his/her suggestion anything else needed to achieve sexy, drop dead gorgeous hair should be suggested and offered. Once the suggestion has been made all the stylist has to say is this…

"Would you like me to do the color for you at the same time?" If the client agrees a price must be agreed and then carry on. To encourage the new client to have the color there and then always offer some discount. Remember this client over 3-years is worth a lot of money to you – don't let this opportunity slip by.

Before the stylist starts they should make sure that the client agrees and gives the go ahead to do what has been suggested.

Now none of the above questions have to be asked in strict order. The questions are simply a guide but you must ask the questions if you want to really take part in SALON SAMPLER to its best effect.

The SAMPLER consultation is a critical part of SALON SAMPLER and you as the salon owner or manager must make sure this is measured, trained and followed through at all times. I advise every salon owner to track and measure this weekly and sometime daily. Never think a face-to-face twice a year is enough it isn't.

Now the consultation doesn't finish here of course. It is ongoing all the way through the service. At the sink, at the station/unit until the last moment when you ask the client if they are happy and until the moment the client leaves your salon.

The stylist will take the client to the desk, show her what is needed beyond today and say a proper goodbye and thank you for coming to our salon.

Powerful, right? Can you imagine the difference that will make in your salon?

Let me go over some quick points to enforce this again.

Knowing what a consultation is according to SALON SAMPLER and what you want from this.

- Train your team to understand the SALON SAMPLER consultation
- Train your team to do the SALON SAMPLER consultation
- Have a training day to practice the SALON SAMPLER consultation

- Have a group meeting to discuss the SALON SAMPLER consultation
- Listen during the SALON SAMPLER consultation
- Advice during the SALON SAMPLER consultation
- Upsell into color restyle etc. during the SALON SAMPLER consultation

Don't forget a client is scared of coming into your salon but she is there because she wants a change. Will you give her the change? If you do she will spend during the sampler and for years after.

And remember the reason this is the core of SALON SAMPLER is this creates great and strong client relationships. They will love you guys for this and be blown away with a service that is based on caring not just doing.

Don't forget at any stage this all goes back to SALON PUNK EXTREME METHOD and SALON SAMPLER at its core. And the purpose of that is to pack out your stylists in as fast as possible and increasing your salon turnover fast! It's about making sure that they have 250 clients (the number of clients any stylists need in their column per year to stay busy) in their personal records and ready to pack out their salon columns week in, week out years after year.

Don't lose focus. This will take some work but it isn't really that hard to do.

We will talk more about the consultation and the critical part it plays in SALON SAMPLER a little bit further down but for now let's carry on.

Practice the SALON SAMPLER consultation and watch them practice

This is without a doubt the most critical part of your SALON SAMPLER. You must practice, practice and practice the consultation until it is perfected to the most perfect state possible.

The SALON SAMPLER consultation is designed to

- Win over a new client forever (what are you doing different?)
- Give your clients an amazing experience (Is your salon really any different to other salons?)
- Create even better hairdressing (train, practice, perfect your work)
- Create new loyal fans of your salon (Fans love new things that are different or one step ahead – are you?)

- Get reviews online (possibly the most critical element of building columns today)
- Generate even more sales (a sample client is for life not for one visit)
- Increase services
- Increase visits
- Increase spends
- Take your salon to a whole new level (if you want to?)

When I had new stylists coming to my salon from other salons I can tell you this most didn't want to do the consultation the way I trained them to do. Why? Hairdressers by their creative nature feel they are stars in their own right and can be lazy – not all – but generally. That isn't meant to be controversial or ignorant. It is based on salon owner feedback and my own 20 years as a salon owner.

Interestingly recently I spoke at a large gathering for around 70 salon owners. The older guys were all speaking about the days when they were (and some still do) 15-20 clients or more per day. I remember that well and it was a killer. They also mention that they have stylist that think doing 15-20 per week is just mad busy. It isn't and it isn't a full column. How things can change. However, most staff love being busy in my experience.

To be a great hairdresser you have to do great things and doing great things starts with clients at the consultation level. Why? Get this part of your service right and you'll blow the clients away. Get this part right and I promise your clients won't ask the price – they'll just pay. I should know I have seen it and done it with myself and with many hundreds of stylists.

Remember average can only create average.

Greatness creates greatness.

How great is your SALON SAMPLER consultation going to be?

First, you'd better know how this works or you're screwed. Make sure (please please please) make sure you have this in place and know exactly how a consultation works.

Here's an example

My knee isn't as good as it used to be so I eventually decided to get it looked at. One practitioner I went to touched it, asked where the pain was and said take anti-inflammatory pills to reduce the pain. That was it. I had the same experienced repeated at the next doctor I went to. In fact, he said it's age!

Finally, I decided to go and try acupuncture. I arrived at the clinic only to be met by a very tall Chinese guy that had married a very small Scottish woman and settled in Manchester, UK. Next, he took me into his consulting room, sat down facing me and started to talk. He explained that it's easier if he asks me in English but writes his notes in Chinese as it's easier for him that way and of course I don't speak Chinese.

Before anything was offered he spoke to me and asked me questions that probably took around twenty minutes easily. He took my pulse, my blood pressures and then eventually asked me to undress and lie on the table where he carefully turned me from a human to a human porcupine. I lay there for 30 minutes with calming music (noises) playing until he came back and removed the pins. I never asked the price. I just paid and it was worth every penny for the experience healing.

Now you have to remember most hairdressers DO NOT carry out a true consultation. Most will have no idea about SAMPLING so you have a huge, huge advantage over all of them just as my acupuncture practitioner has over his competition just like you will have.

So here it is again but remember the consultation really starts when the client first gets in touch with your salon and that is way before this actual face-to-face.

This is The SALON SAMPLER consultation

I just got back from my dentist. He is a new dentist for me so I was very nervous. I told him about my crown and how the tooth underneath was hurting me. He listened for a while, touched and play around in my mouth. Took an x-ray and then sat me up again.

This first part of my consultation took around 30-minues. He then carefully went through the options I had before me, sowed me the x-ray and all the other issues I had. The big option was I had to replace the crown and remove a root of a tooth. It was going to cost me £1,400. I said ok, and booked my next appointment.

I can share this with you. I had been to another dentist that I didn't go back to for the same problem because the consultation was almost non-existent. The reason I said yes to this one was his consultation was very thorough and I felt absolutely confident that he had my best interested at heart.

I took my wife into a very famous hair salon for advice. She has wonderfully thick, wavy dark hair. When we walked through the salon front door a stylist was leaning on the door frame, smoking and scrolling. Once inside we had to sit down and wait and wait and wait and wait. The BEST stylist in the salon finally came over. It was the same guy now stinking of cigarettes from the front door. I think we had to wait whilst he logged in, checked out, liked, commented and uploaded. Anyway … my wife really wanted advice. He simply stood behind the chair and asked her what she wanted. She replied that I need advice. He replied advice on what? She told him about her hair and any other hair issues and he simply replied, 'I can trim it if you like.' The price was £95 in Manchester, U.K.

NO THANKS … we just got up and left!

You really need to think about your consultation and know what you want from the consultation. Do not forget this is not a robotic process. This is all about showing how much you care about the client and her hair. The following is a guide. I'd suggest sticking closely to it at first and then later if needed it can change slightly as long as you stick to the guidelines.

BIG REMINDER: The purpose of this SALON SAMPLER consultation is to get your salon columns packed out every day and to win over the new client. The other purpose is to increase the average spend of your salon clients and sell more services or retail. The OTHER AND MOST IMPORTANT reason is to get them and keep them as a new client that is happy with you and happy to refer friends to you also.

There is no other purpose than this. Make sure your new stylists understand and get it.

Three magic words you and your stylist must commit and remember

1. Practice
2. Practice
3. Practice

Let's get started on the actual consultation itself. This has been done in bullet notes so you can remember easier so make it more a conversation once you practice.

Once your new client comes into your salon approach the client and shakes hand with you – smile. This will break down any barriers and nerves right away and makes the client feel at ease.

Introduce yourself right away, tell her your name right away and ask her name or even better know her name (it's in the book). Again this removes barriers once we know name of each other.

Use her name as soon as you speak to her but don't overdo it keep it informal but friendly. Once again, another barrier breaker, keeps the client feeling relaxed and more comfortable. Now she is with a friend rather than a new salon.

Walk her over to your styling unit and show her exactly where to sit. Place a hand on her back or shoulder just make her comfortable. This reveals a caring side rather than a standing behind the chair lazy side.

Turn the chair for her to sit on and direct her with your hand to the seat. The closeness can make her feel nervous again so be aware and make it all feel as natural as possible. Place a hand on her shoulder (if it's natural) and ask if she is comfortable.

Sit down at eye level with her and chat with her NOT at her. This removes the superior complex that can happen when someone speaks down to you. This way you are chatting with her rather than speaking at her.

So far, she will be impressed and want more rather than feel terrified. This is the power for a strong sampler consultation and the power of relaxing a client. A more relaxed client will not only take your advice but – spend more!

Now ask; does she have any specific problems with hair (hair frizzy, flat etc). Her previous stylist won't be solving any hair issues they will simply be doing her hair like the usually do it. Find a problem and fix that problem. EVERY client has a problem with their hair they try to ignore. Most clients also want a restyle that is a fact. It could be their existing stylist never restyles their hair. Ask as much as you can and be open to the reply.

Does she have any idea what she wants today? Probably not so you must do your best to tease it out from her. If she fails to say this is where you MUST advise her.

Would she like a ton of hair advice? Of course, clients always want advice but they rarely ask. Tell them everything you can tell them that will take their hair from what it is not to just amazing.

Listen very attentively. Ask a question and allow her to reply in full. Do not break her flow just allow her to keep speaking and you must listen. You are listening out for hair problems to solve.

Then and only then, offer the perfect solution to her annoying hair problem. If she needs balayage, products or just a new brush, make sure you advise her. Own the conversation and own your advice. This will make you stand-out as an expert. This will create a stronger client that will remain loyal after all she won't get this advice anywhere else.

Agree with her to create that perfect hair solution. Don't just tell her what you are doing, make sure you get her to agree with you.

Tell her and go over exactly what you are going to be doing to her hair and ask if she agrees. You need her to agree or at least agree that she trusts your advice.

Walk her to sink area and introduce backwash assistant by name. This again breaks down barriers. I used to always warn my backwash assistant and remind her to go over-the-top with any service at the backwash. Including things like Olaplex or PCC from Le Biosthetique. Good service, low cost and massive return.

Get your assistant to do backwash consultation. She won't be getting this at her salon now so make sure it's done perfect. (if you allow a new junior here that is going to soak her blouse and fail to rinse of all of the conditioner – you are screwed) Keep the standard high all the way through.

Advise on condition and use right products. The assistant should have the knowledge to advice correctly. Tell her the exact products that will help her once she leaves the salon.

Bring the client back to stylist position. This is your opportunity to shine. Lay it all on as thick, hard and over-the-top as possible.

Tell her from start to end what you are doing and agree as you go along. She will be wondering so just tell her. Your style will probably be different to her previous hairdresser. Telling her reassures her all along.

YOU must control the service all the way through even if the client resists she is NOT a hairdresser – stay in control. If she tells you to do something another way be polite and reassure her that you know what is best.

Talk to her from beginning to end but be light not intense. Do not use robot conversation like, "are you going out tonight", or "have you booked a holiday?". Be interesting and interested. Some clients don't want to talk and that is fine.

Try to avoid the usual bland questions like, holidays, going out tonight and all that bland questioning that most clients really don't enjoy.

Don't spend two hours talking about yourself and your life – they don't care! And if you do, they won't be back.

Show her how to dry her hair for home care. She'll be impressed after all do you really think she'll just be able to do it? No so show her.

Let the client have a go at drying her own hair with you. And show how to apply your salon products.

Let her have a go at applying products and show her the right amount. Put them in her hand and let her see the amount. Clients love to use half a bottle of product in one spot and then wonder why it didn't work. Show her what to do and why you do it.

You must ask her at the end if she really is happy with finish, the way it looks and her new image?

Ask if there is anything at all you could do that will make her totally in love with her hair.

Tell her she looks amazing, gorgeous, stunning and if it's appropriate kiss her on the cheek. Although these days this might provoke something from nothing so read the situation carefully. Most people are just people so ride with what you feel.

Walk back over to the desk and keep complimenting her new look as you move over there.

Stand facing her and put your fingers in her hair and move it around the same way she would do it if facing her mirror at home. Make sure you have a huge mirror in the reception near the window so she can see her hair in natural light and see how good she looks.

Show her and ask if she'd like to take the products you used on her hair today. If you don't she really will wonder what you used and why you never offered. Even worse she will try and buy something like what you used elsewhere but as you know it'll be nothing like you used.

Repeat any hair hacks she needs to know. Fringe fix, frizz fix, volume fix. Show her how to fix them fast.

Now, explain vouchers etc. in goodie bag and how to use them. You need a gift to complete the SAMPLER service. If you don't have one create one.

Go through how referrals work. And ask her to send people to you. This is the best time as she will feel on a high.

Also ask if she would do any of these before she leaves ...

Leave an online review. You will have to have it open and set up to do this fast.

Tag a friend

Salon selfie

Hash tag/@ Instagram/facebook/social.

Tell her exactly how her reward for sending you a new client.

Ask for a rebooking.

Then thank her for her business.

Tell her next time maybe you will do this that or the other.

See her out of the salon door.

Now your new stylist has practiced this with a real person for an hour or so you must get them to agree and confirm they fully understand the consultation process.

Now you want this to look really slick? Set a small exam at the end of this and ask your new stylist maybe 10-12 questions from the consultation process above.

Of course, you'll need to explain to them the SALON SAMPLER column building processes also.

Here are a few more things you really must double check at this stage with stylists before they can create a really amazing SAMPLING session in your salon.

- Do they know and understand all of your products?
- Do they know and understand all of your retail products?
- Do they understand how the salon works and reception?

- Do they really understand what you expect from them?

I'll keep on saying this… This is all about blowing a new client away during a SAMPLER. It needs work, commitment and dedication with planning. You must commit to doing this.

Do this with your sampler stylist

- Sit with your stylist in a quiet place
- Go through the reason for the SALON SAMPLER consultation
- Explain it in all the details you've read
- Make sure they fully understand
- Practice the consultation
- Be flexible with the bullet points above
- Watch them carefully practice
- Be kind and guide them
- Praise them but tell them where they also go wrong
- Be brave and stand up for your salon ethics

- Make sure they understand your salon ethos and ideal or even manifesto
- Tell them this will make them better stylists with a more loyal following
- Tell them they will earn more. Explain how the earnings work
- Tell them clients will love it because they really will rave about this
- Tell them this is going to make them even more amazing

Stand up and be counted, this is your salon and your salon only, no one will do it for you. Everything is possible, make it work.

I cannot emphasise enough the power of the SAMPLER CONSULTATION. If this doesn't get done you will struggle. This is the toughest bit to crack but I want to encourage you to work on it, don't give up on it and I promise it'll be worth every effort.

Final note: PRACTICE until the tips of your fingers are raw.

SALON SAMPLER DISTRIBUTION PROCESS

First there are mistakes salons make with FREE sample programs. I want to share with you the biggest so you can see and know what to avoid.

Handing out vouchers to just anyone hoping they will come into the salon. One salon complained they started getting one or two homeless into their salon from FREE haircuts. Well you can't blame the homeless! Don't hand them out to just anyone.

Putting FREE in a newspaper. Do this and you will be inundated with a surge of clients you will never see again after the free appointment.

Sending free by text, email or in a letter. What client will want to pay after they see this. Big mistake.

Splashing free all over social media. You will lower the perception of your salon and again be run off your feet from free requests.

Giving free vouchers to regular clients is just … INSANE – don't do it!

Handing out FREE vouchers or SAMPLES to anyone and everyone will destroy your salon business and decimate columns.

It is critical to make sure they get handed out properly.

This is not about volume, it is about targeting potential clients that will come again if we do everything right.

It is better to hand out just 5 and get all five back rather than hand out 1000 and get the wrong clients back.

The sampling distribution process

Every modern-day 'expert' insists on doing everything with an iPhone or digital. This is the worst way to do sampler. We have to be far more direct with SAMPLER.

IMPORTANT: Paper or card vouchers will always give you a bigger result than anything else. I advise as part of SALON SAMPLER you use only flyers of vouchers that go into someone's hand – NOT digital.

You now have the consultation right and have practiced and perfected it. Now the vouchers must go out – the SALON SAMPLES.

Here is the best process that is proven to work.

First decide which member of staff will be doing salon sampler. NEVER run all the team – just one at a time. Control is the key here.

Go through the whole process and remind them of the outcome – to win a client for life. Allocate a certain number of vouchers. If they are given ten you must check at the end of the day that all ten have been handed out. If only nine have gone out – why?

The stylist should then go out of the salon and target potential clients.

Someone that looks like a potential client… that is a personal choice. Let's say you have a young stylist that loves doing short, quirky, young hairdressing. Well that stylist would target exactly that kind of client.

They should know who they want as clients because let's be honest we all know who we don't want as clients.

The stylist should leave the salon and approach those targets like this.

"Excuse me, sorry to bother you, I am a senior stylist from XZY hair. I love your hair and would love to offer you a free sample or free cut and design with me. When would you like to come in?"

If the person says no thanks – move on.

If she says yes great make sure you work your dates and even phone the salon there and then.

If the stylist is very quiet well I would allow a client in at any time. If the stylist is just topping up their column with some new clients, be selective. In other words, if she is already booked out on Saturday don't allow a free slot to go into a paying slot.

Just be sensible.

The flyer should have an expiry date no longer than 3-days later. Same day is your strongest option. The reason is, if we leave it open you might be taking on free appointments six months later when the stylist is jam packed. Remember control is the key.

If no one is on the streets target shops where you will find haircuts you want to take on. For example, the stylist could go into a cool clothes shop and find the manager or just go to the desk and speak to staff (not customers). Tell them again who you are, where you are from and you are having an open night (time period) where you are offering some free samples of hairdressing. You'd love them all to come in. Ask when they would like to come in?

Again, write of the vouchers and make sure they are dated no longer than three days ahead.

In other words, …

- Find the right people you want in your salon.

- Do a small script/speech to approach them.
- Ask for the appointment.
- Hand them the flyer with their name, your name and an expiry date.

THE BIG KEY is track and measure everything. In other words, if they give out five flyers you should be getting a minimum of one back. If they get none back there is a problem. They are probably handing them out to the wrong clients or not doing the script when they approach them or even worse – just handing the flyers to anyone and everyone.

Track and measure everything.

When the client arrives at the salon.

Of course, we have our SALON SAMPLER consultation but it is critical this is a visit the new client doesn't forget.

And that's it.

Finally, is this worth the hassle?

Look at this.

Every new client is preprogrammed to spend more. They come because they want a change. This means whatever is advised – if done well – they will go for.

I did this exact process with a new stylist that had zero clients in his column when he began. His averages were just £23 per client doing what he always did. After doing SALON SAMPLER with him his average bill went from £23 per client to £171 per client. Not a single free sample client actually had free hairdressing. Yes they had a free haircut but they paid for colour, retail, and other services.

Like I said right at the start…

"there is no such thing as free"

Even better if one client spends £171 each visit and visits your salon just five visits per year that is a huge £855 from just one client.

If you pull in one hundred new clients from SALON SAMPLER and they spend the same as above that means you've increased your salon takings by a massive £85,500. From just 100 new clients.

I have had salons pull in **over sixty new clients per week** on SAMPLING.

Do your numbers.

Here it is all again.

- The understanding
- The consultation
- The process

This is easy, you really can do this.

What goes on your SALON SAMPLER flyer?

The design should be kept simple.

FREE CUT & FINISH

*This is your **<u>FREE haircut at a No.1 salon</u>**. You have 36 hours to use it. Your top stylist's name is below.*

Usual price £42 you pay ZERO... Absolutely free.

*Includes: **FREE** consultation, **FREE** restyle advice, **FREE** colour advice, **FREE** refreshments, **FREE** treatments and TOP STYLIST for **FREE**.*

Stylist Name: Expires:

Salon name and address, contact details

Terms and conditions should go at the bottom or the back of the voucher

---

If I was opening a new salon this tomorrow ...

If I was opening a new salon tomorrow this would be my only focus because I know when sampling is done properly, it is fast, very fast. This is a tool that when done properly no one can resist. I have seen insane numbers pile into salons and columns using just this.

The big issue we have in our industry is we are and have always been driven by fads and the latest things. The killer I have seen is allowing software or marketing or promotional companies to take control of marketing your salon. This is a huge mistake.

SALON SAMPLER is salon direct marketing in its purest form. It takes you away from the technicalities of the computer screen and allows you to engage once more with real people. It allows you to see, speak, hear, smell and communicate at a very human level and very human touch.

It is the perfect punk way of marketing. In other words, going against the grain and doing the exact opposite to what all other salons are doing.

And then there is this. Don't give up. Practice the system, keep trying, keep manipulating and making the tweaks, changes and adjustments until you get it right. This is marketing at is very best. This is results and costs as low and as high as they will go. But you must never give up.

I'd love to know how you get on so please use our social media to let us know.

The Salon Punk

Alan Forrest Smith

About Alan Forrest Smith & SalonPunk.com

Hairdressing is in my blood. I can't escape regardless of how many times I might have tried.

I love it.

I hate it.

I love it.

Today I live in between Manchester, U.K. and Tbilisi in the Republic of Georgia (next to Turkey and Russia) with my wife Tamuna.

Since selling my salons I have always been involved with hairdressing salons at many levels. Apart from the hairdressing industry I have worked with literally hundreds of new businesses, old businesses, corporate businesses, startups, struggling and business that just demand more. Most of this work is done through my other site at www.OrangeBeetle.com where I built a strong reputation as being an experts-expert in more results and response.

Also I write fulltime as a published author of many books on philosophy, business and breakthrough topics such as finding happiness.

Salon Punk© is a child I adore. I love helping salon owners create happier places to work and service their community.

Hair is the most wonderful of things. It can create a smile or enrage tears. I will never underestimate that power.

So to finish here is a few things you might not know about me.

I lost my big adult front teeth at the age of ten when I fell over whilst wearing a large brown paper potato sack from head to toe and landing on my face.

I saved a man's life on a beach in Spain. He had drowned and I pulled him out, gave him the kiss of life and he came back to life!

I proposed to my wife early one morning in bed and said to her… 'Shall we go buy a ring then book a flight to New York? She asked why and I replied… 'Marry me'. She said 'yes' (thank god!)

I once saw a vision of a giant whilst with a Shaman in the Amazon forest in Ecuador (TRUE).

I once lost everything I ever owned in my life through a catastrophic divorce as recent as 2010. I was broke, homeless and looked like death! By mid-2010 I had designed a new life that looked exactly like I wanted it to look.

I used to worry about what others thought but eventually realised they were all thinking the same thing. I discovered that the only person I should worry about was myself. If I were fine those around me would be fine.

I love motorbikes.

I love tattoos.

I love my wife.

I love life.

That's it … for now anyway.

Alan Forrest Smith

Here's my other websites.

www.AlanForrestSmith.com

www.OrangeBeetle.com

More From SalonPunk.com

BEST-SELLING PAPERBACK - THE SALON PUNK

NEW PAPERBACK: A Breakthrough Book Packed With Ideas And Experiences You Absolutely Should Know On How To Create The Big Salon Breakthrough You Really Deserve.

Every Salon Owner Should Own This Book ... That Includes You!

www.salonpunk.com or Amazon.com

Salon Extreme21© BEST SELLING SALON BUSINESS MANUAL.

You might just want more ideas on what to do and how to build your salon business. our BEST-SELLING manual Salon Extreme21© (21-days to grow your salon business) does just that. It's almost 500 pages in size, it's a large A4 folder and it is designed to be handled, read, written on and copied for the tons of salon management, salon marketing, salon business building idea. What else can I say apart from salon owners absolutely love it, we ship it all over the globe every week and the feedback is pretty amazing. Order now. The MAX delivery time is 15-days depending on where you are. UK delivery is around one week.

www.salonpunk.com

SALON BUSINESS CONSULTATION: THE EXTREME METHOD@

How about getting your nagging salon problem solved so fast that you will never believe it?

Alan offers unique, bespoke and highly charge consulting calls over any medium you use (Type, WhatsApp etc). Share your most pressing issues and you are pretty much guaranteed to leave the call with a solution that is designed around your salon. One salon owners just recently have now discovered the best path to come off the shop floor and keep her staff packed out at the same time after just 60-minutes with Alan

www.salonpunk.com/services

SALON EXTREME LIVE:

Regardless of how long you've been in business, there are times when you simply want to hear something refreshing, motivating, inspiring and uplifting. All can offer bespoke talks to fit your salon very precisely.

www.salonpunk.com/live

Don't forget YOUR FREE BONUS!

Download FREE copy of ***How to Access and Get Back Missing Salon Clients in 15 Minutes Using Your Smartphone***

Simply visit www.salonpunk.com/imissing

Register your details, name and email address (we need them to send you the free book) and that's it.

Lightning Source UK Ltd.
Milton Keynes UK
UKHW011459250419
341602UK00001B/52/P

9 781513 634470